Fantasia

An Adult Coloring Book Of Fantasy & Mythology

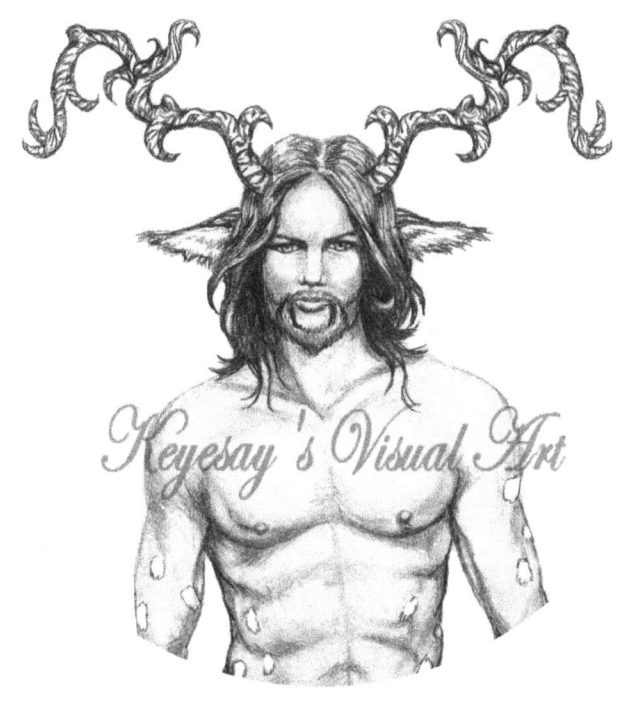

Artwork by Casey "Keyesay" Gilmore

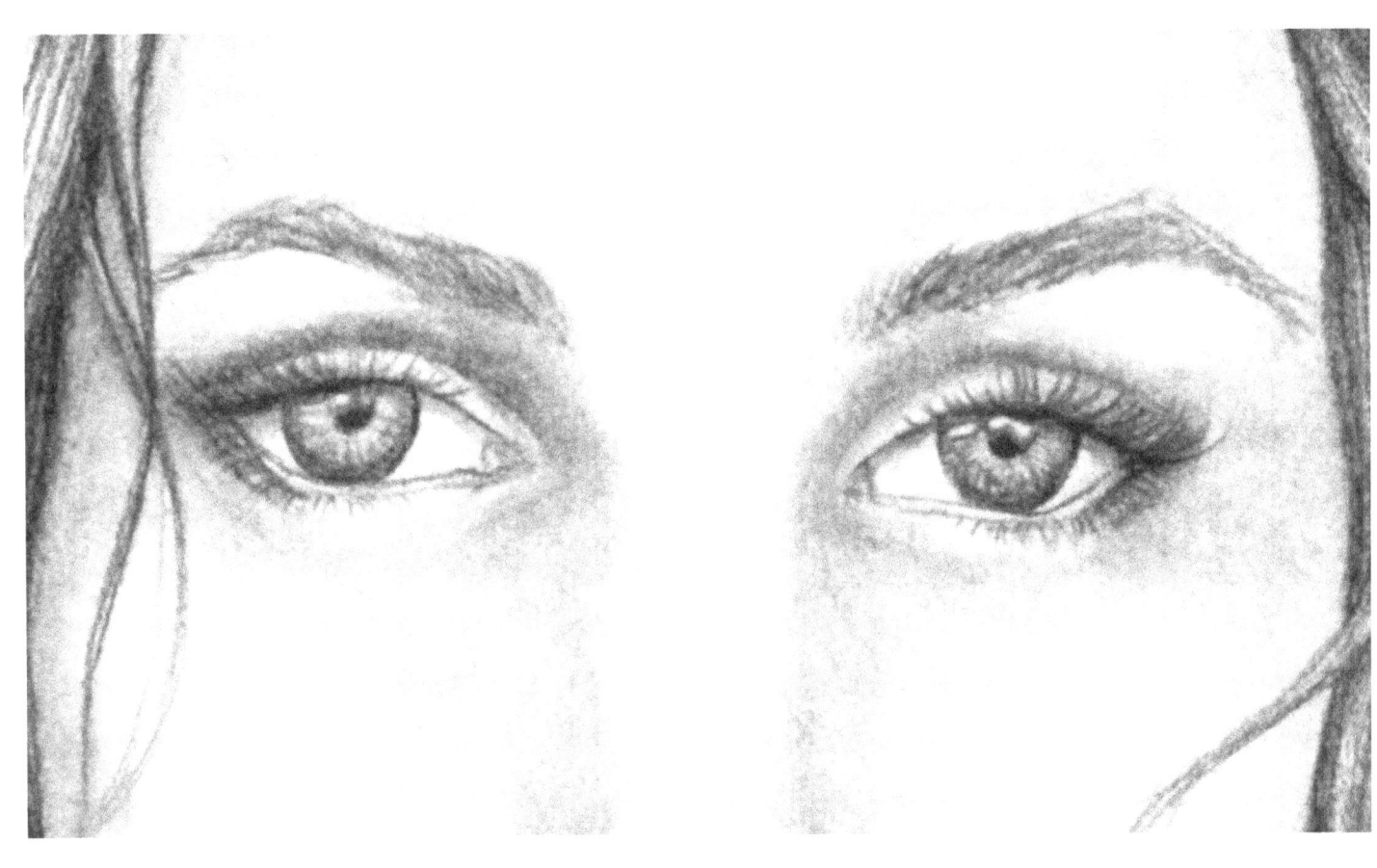

All designs are hand drawn & were comprehensively
selected by Casey to provide a concise
but thorough introduction to

"Fantasia" An Adult Coloring Book of Fantasy and Mythology

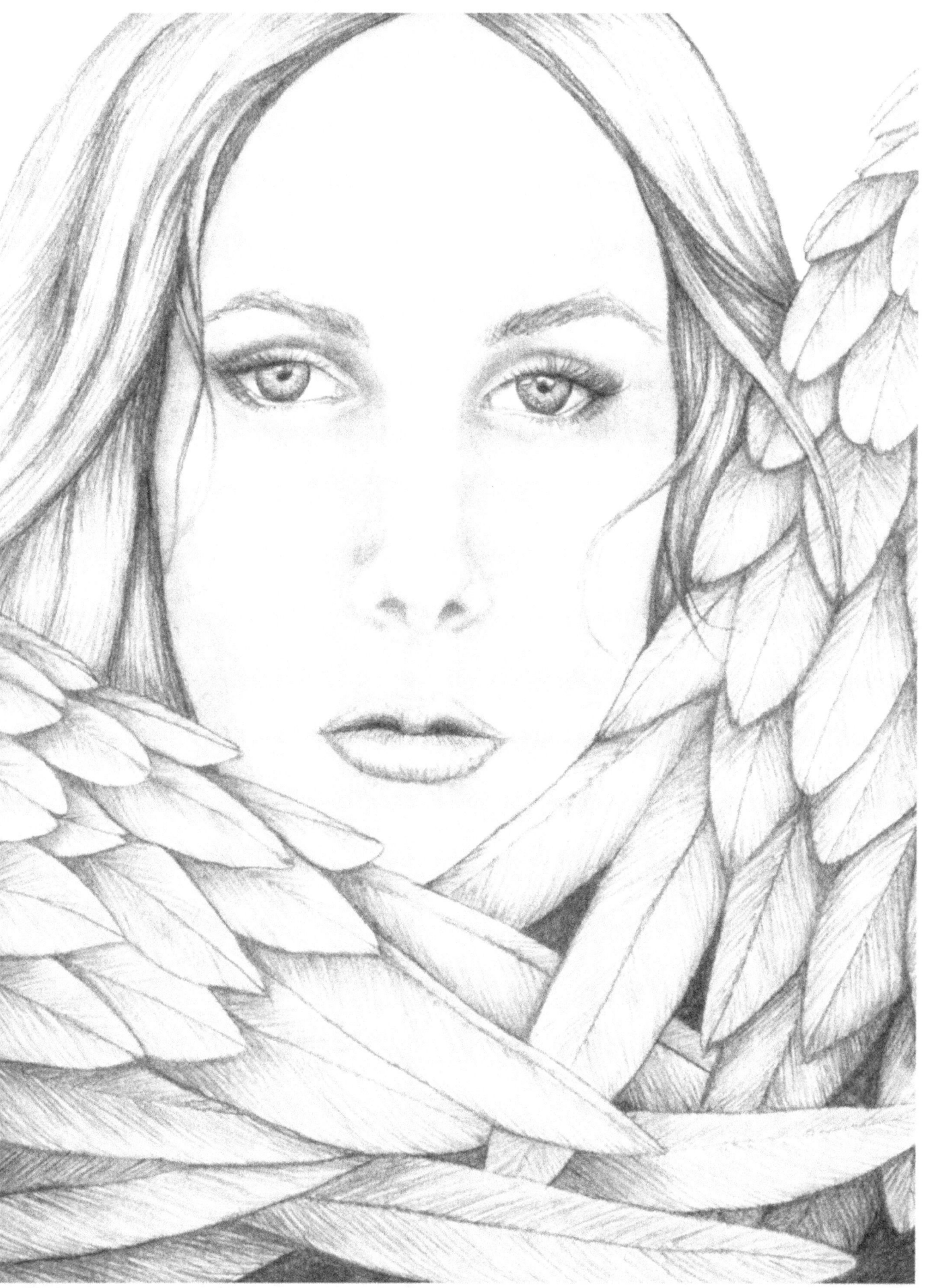

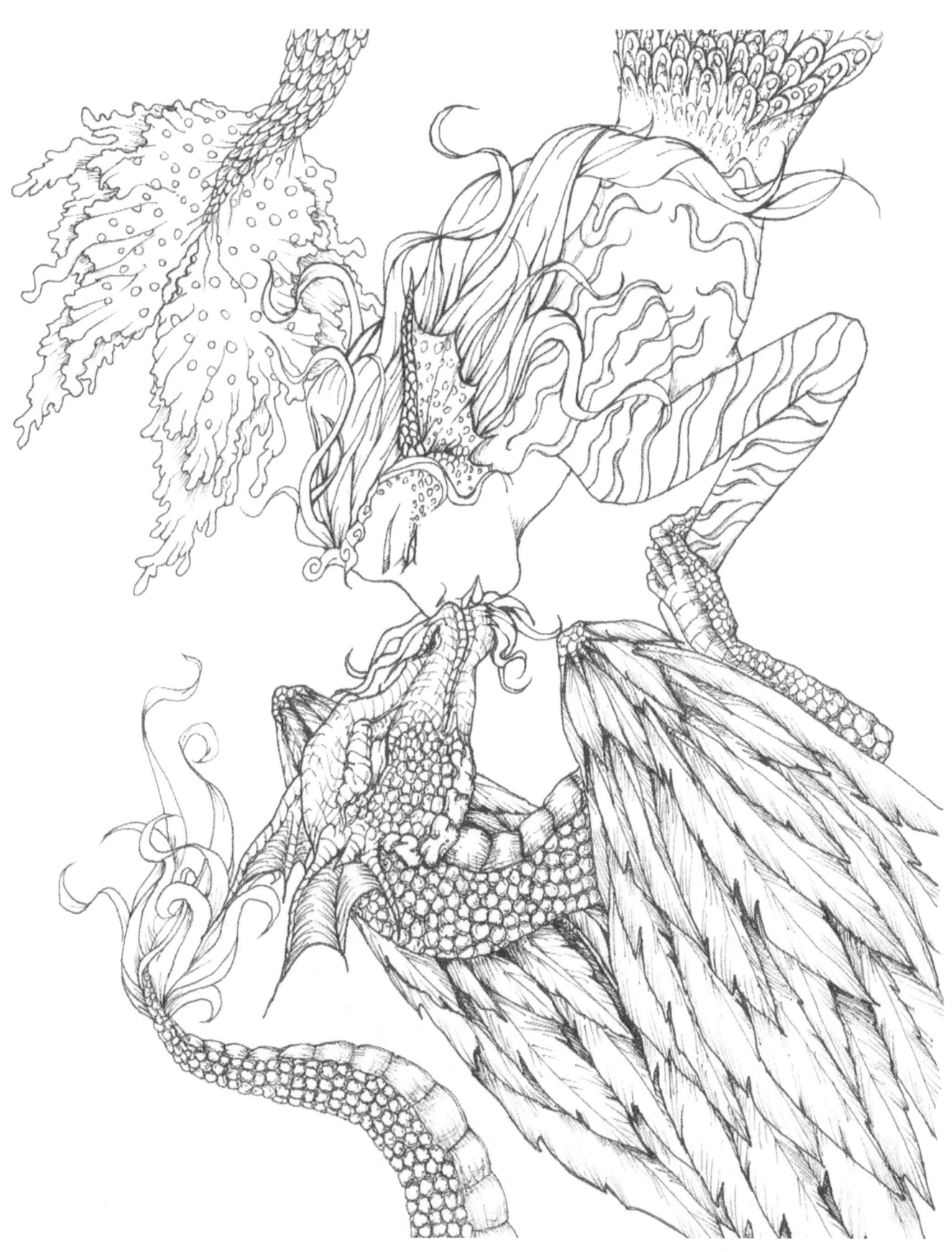

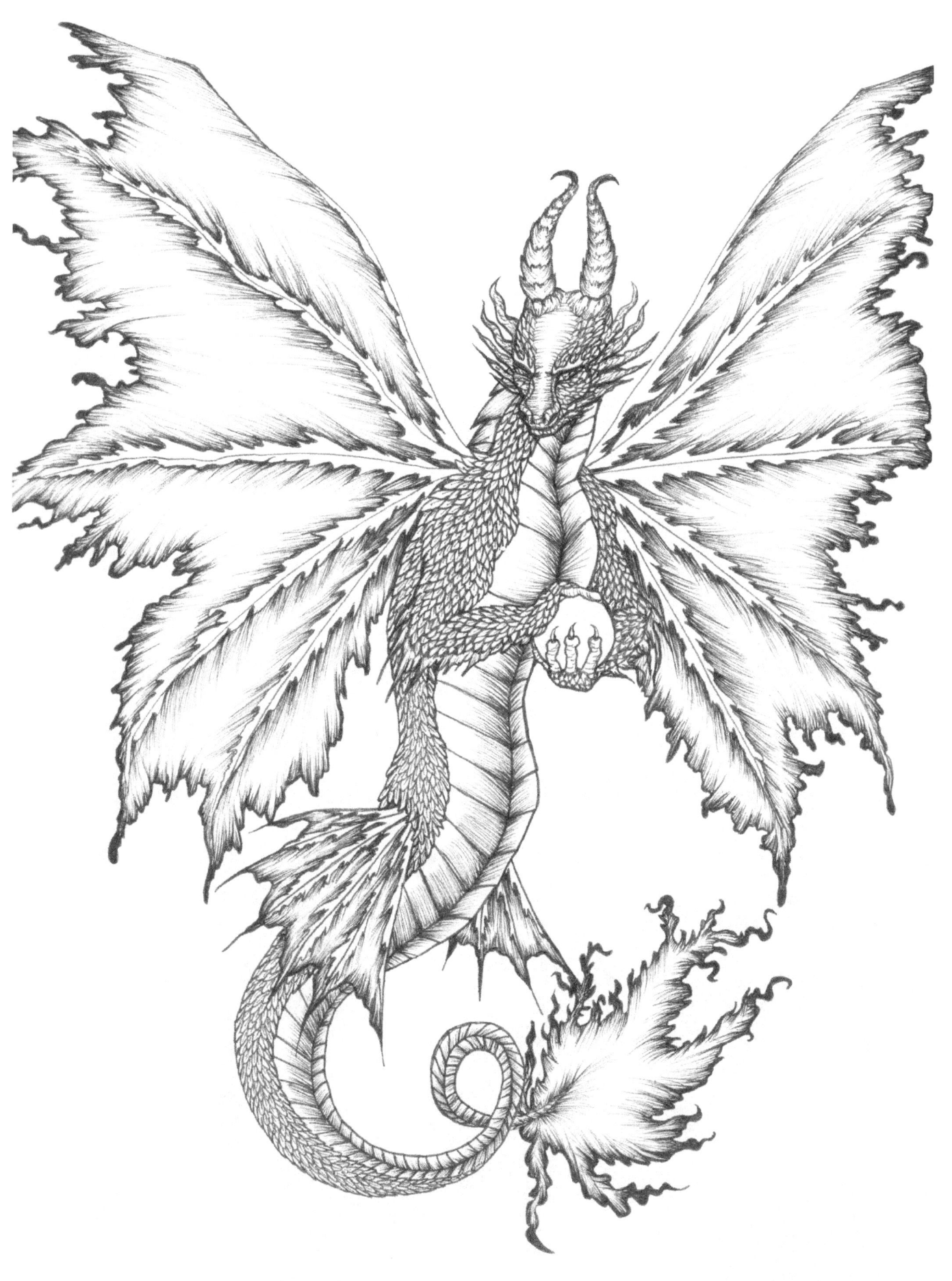

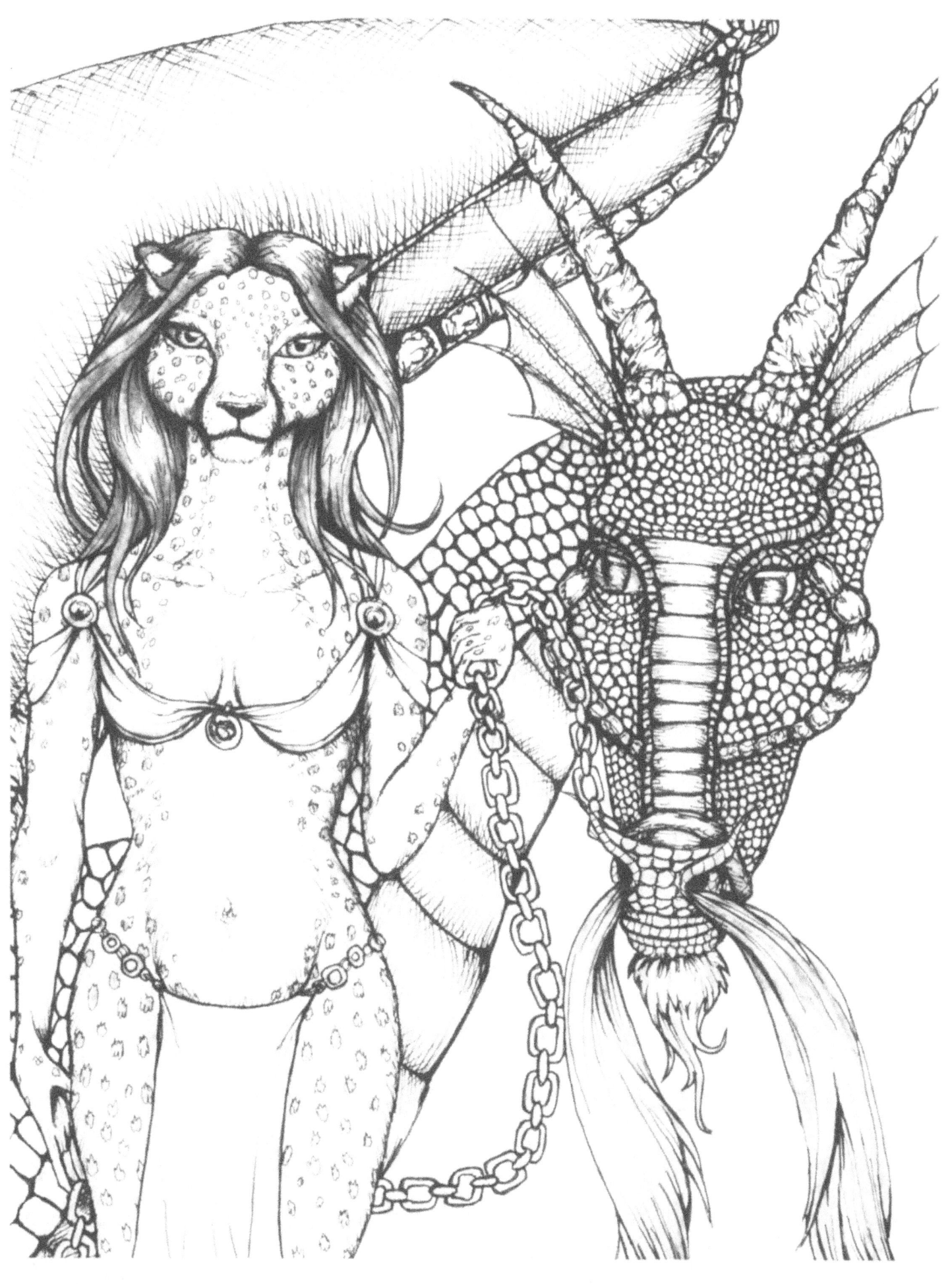

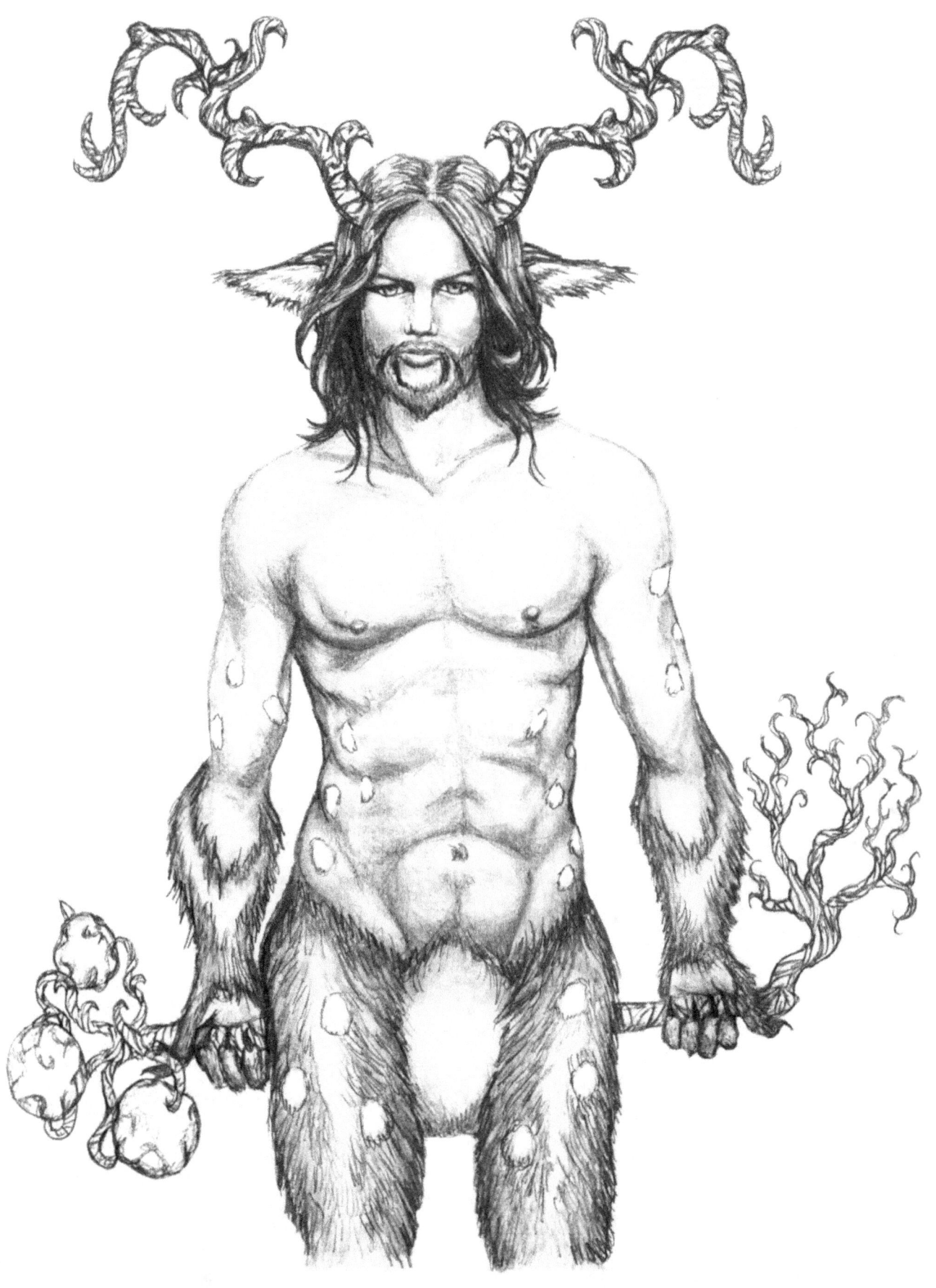

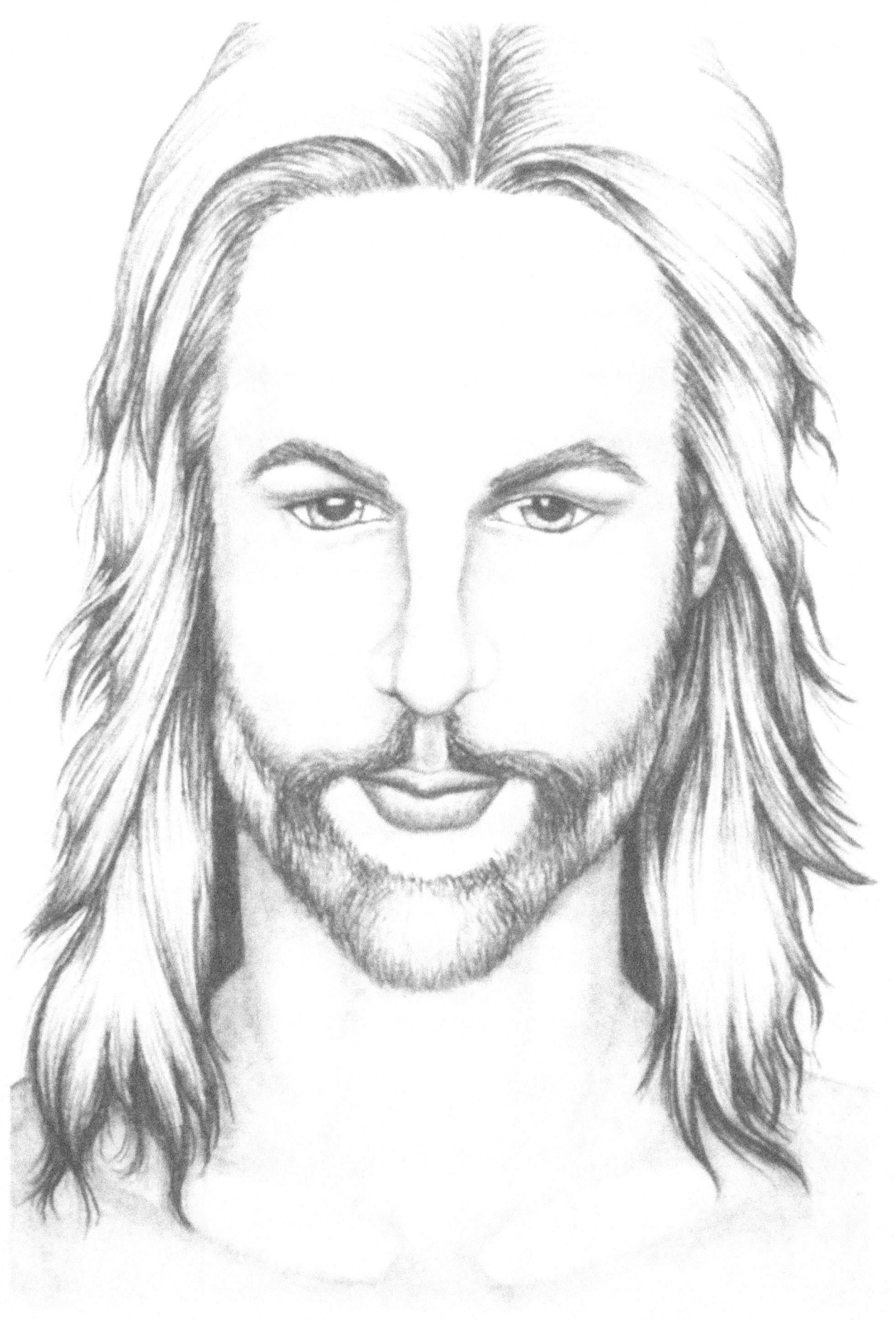

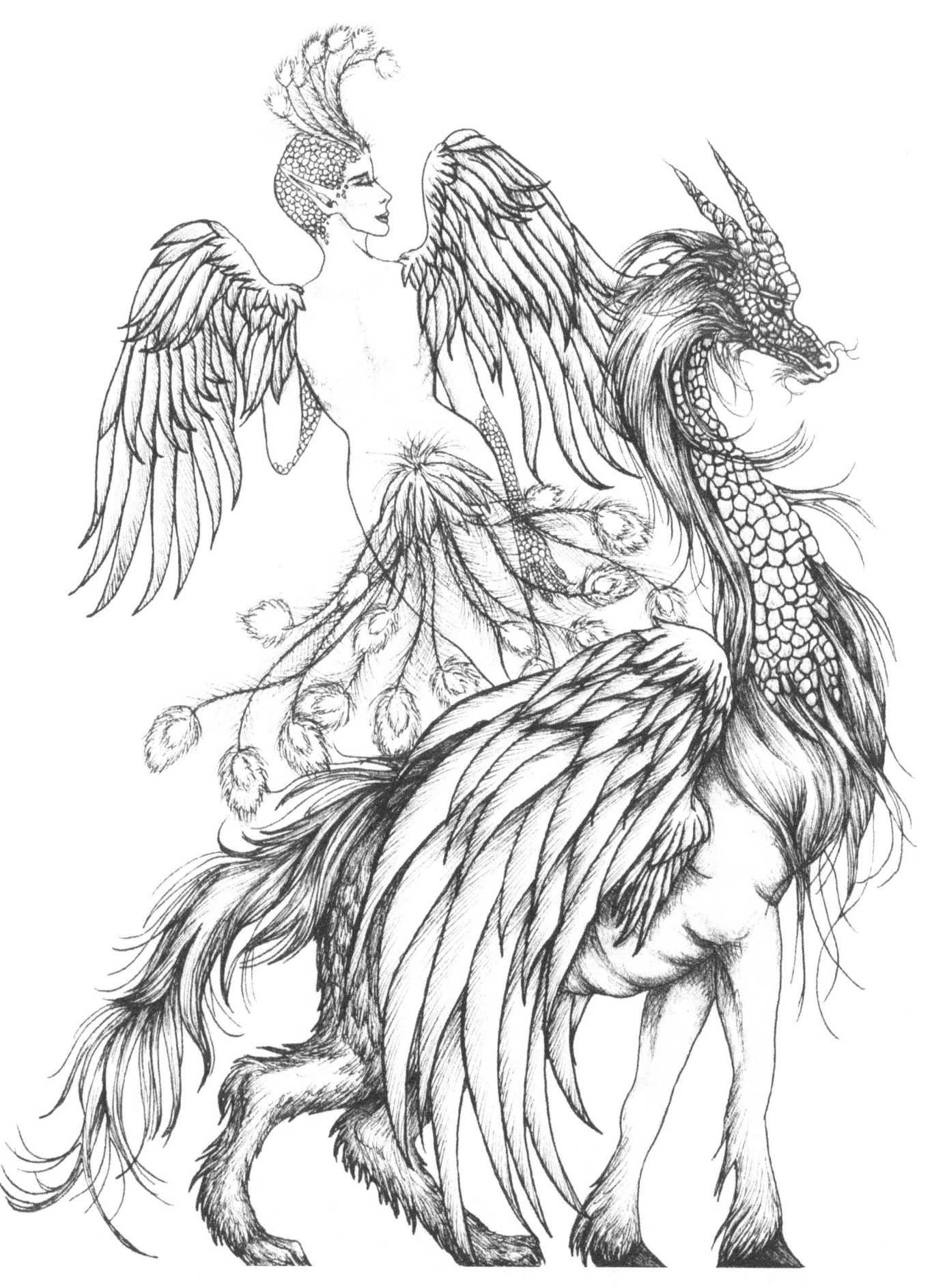

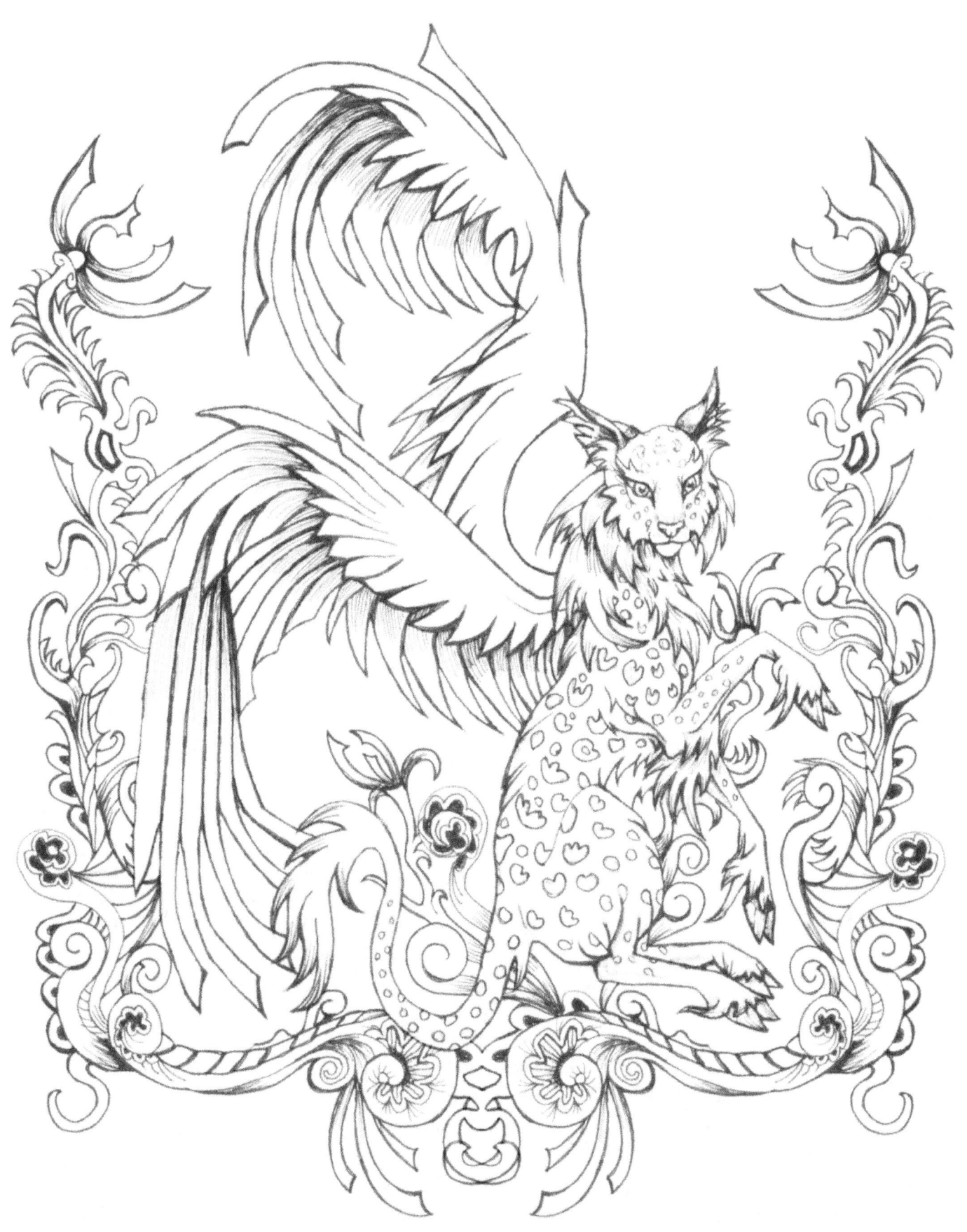

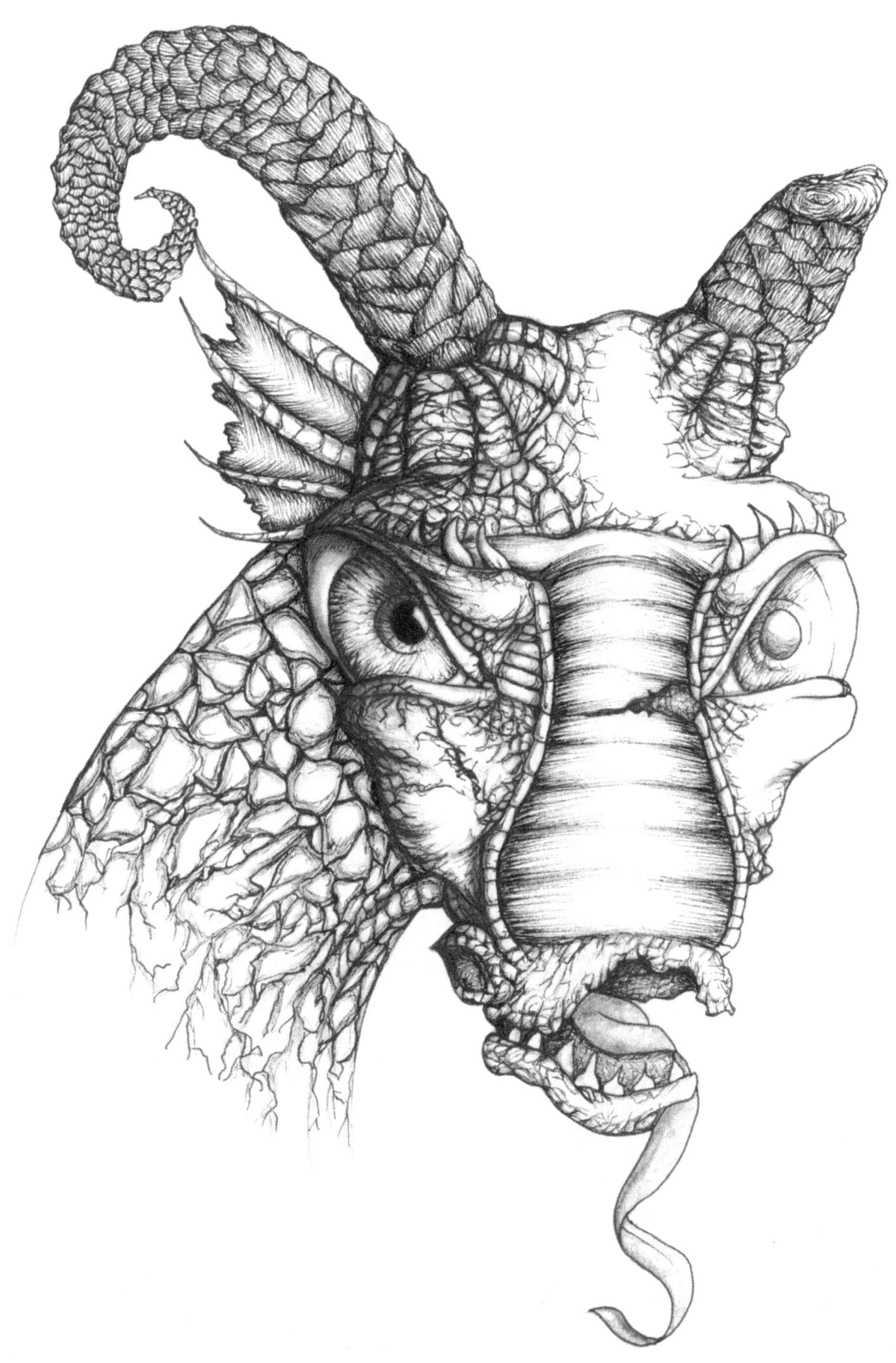

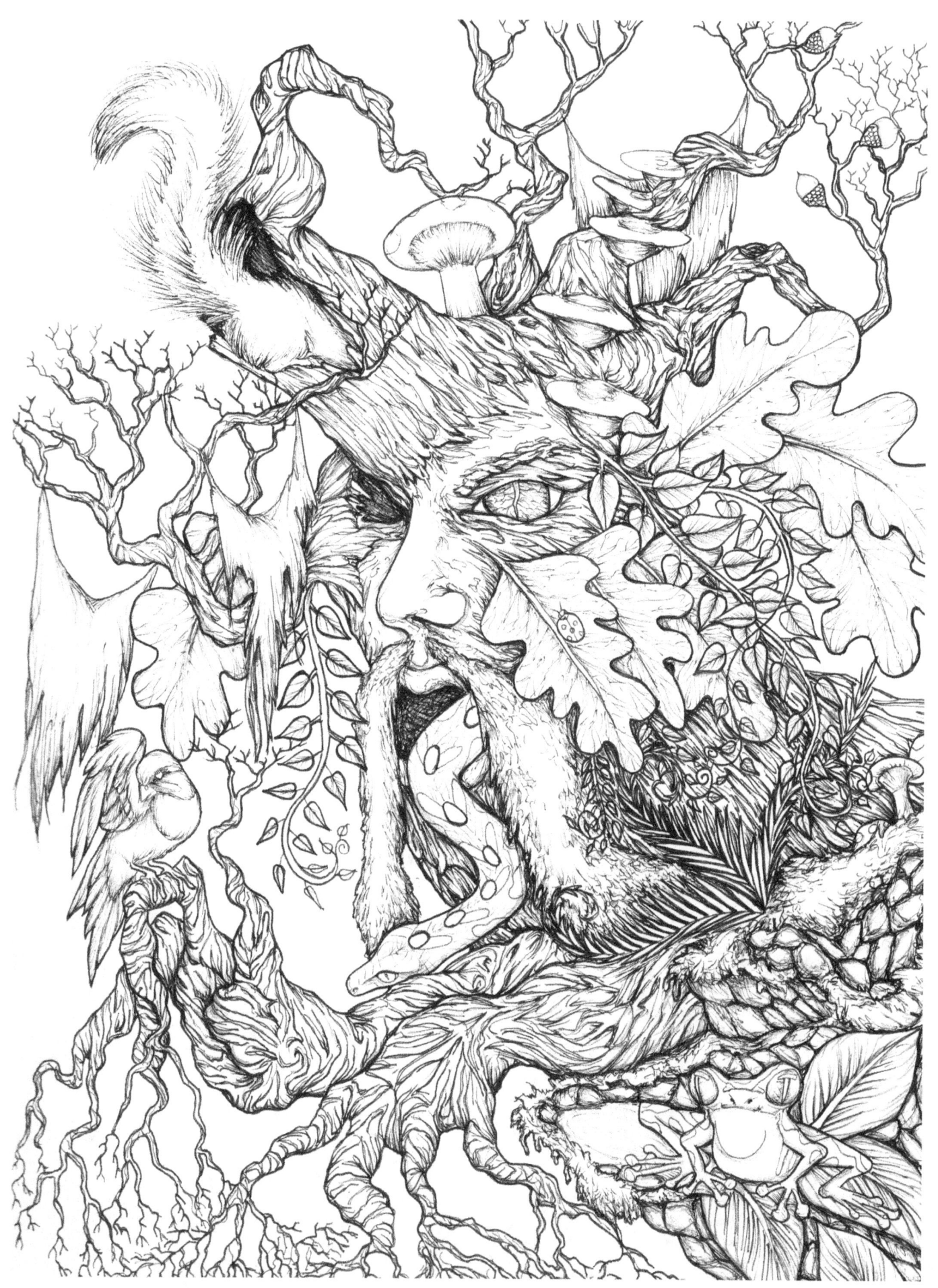

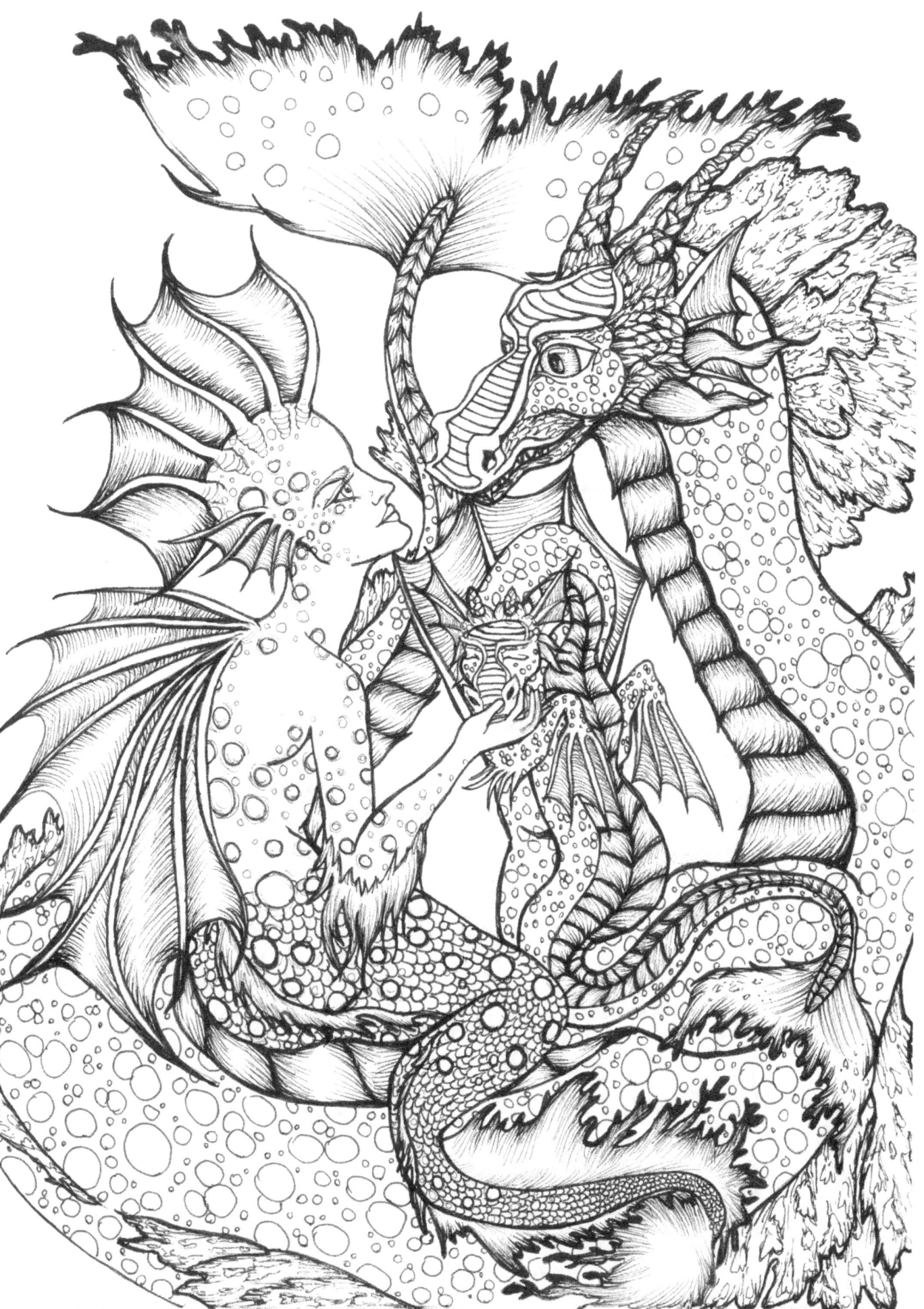

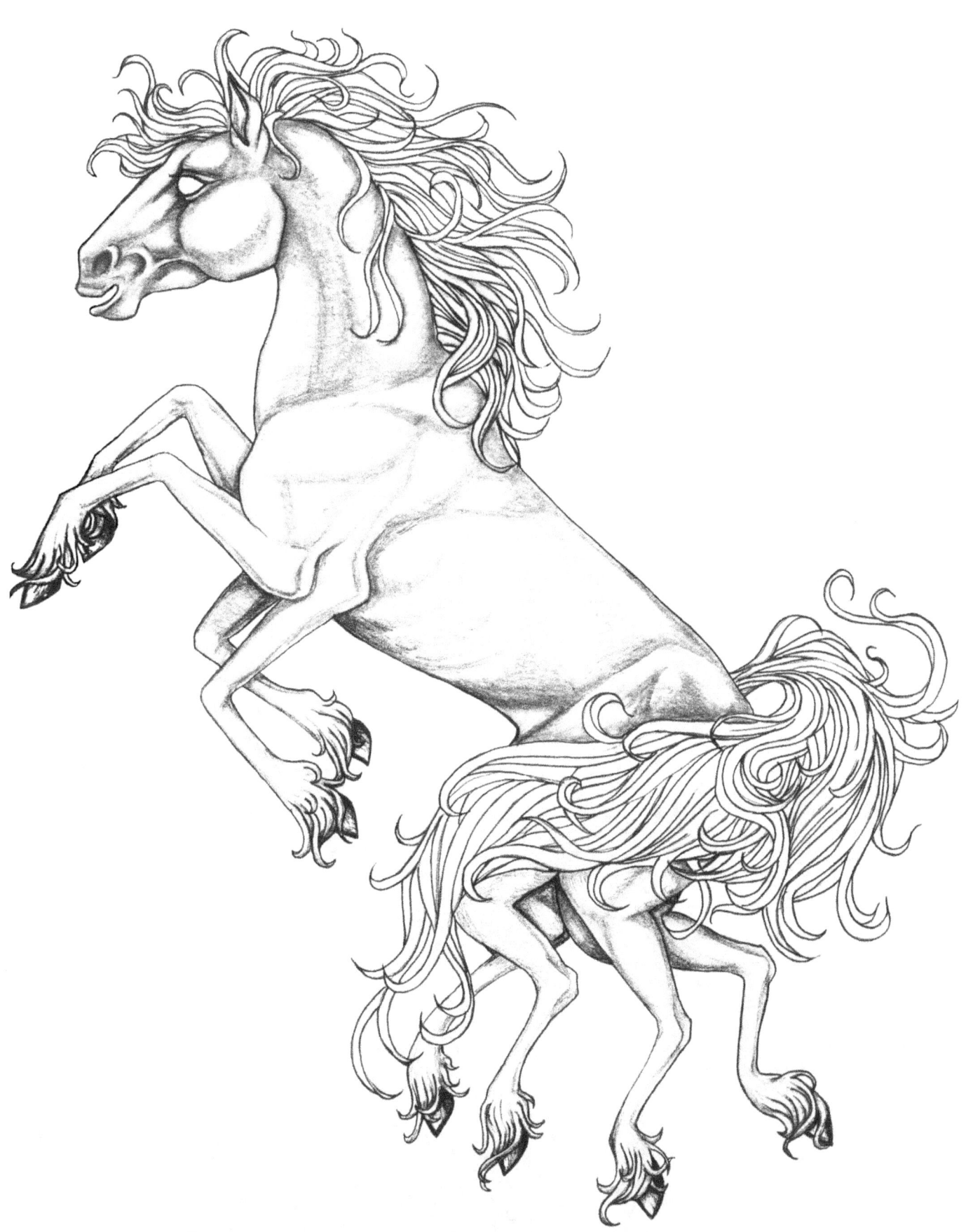

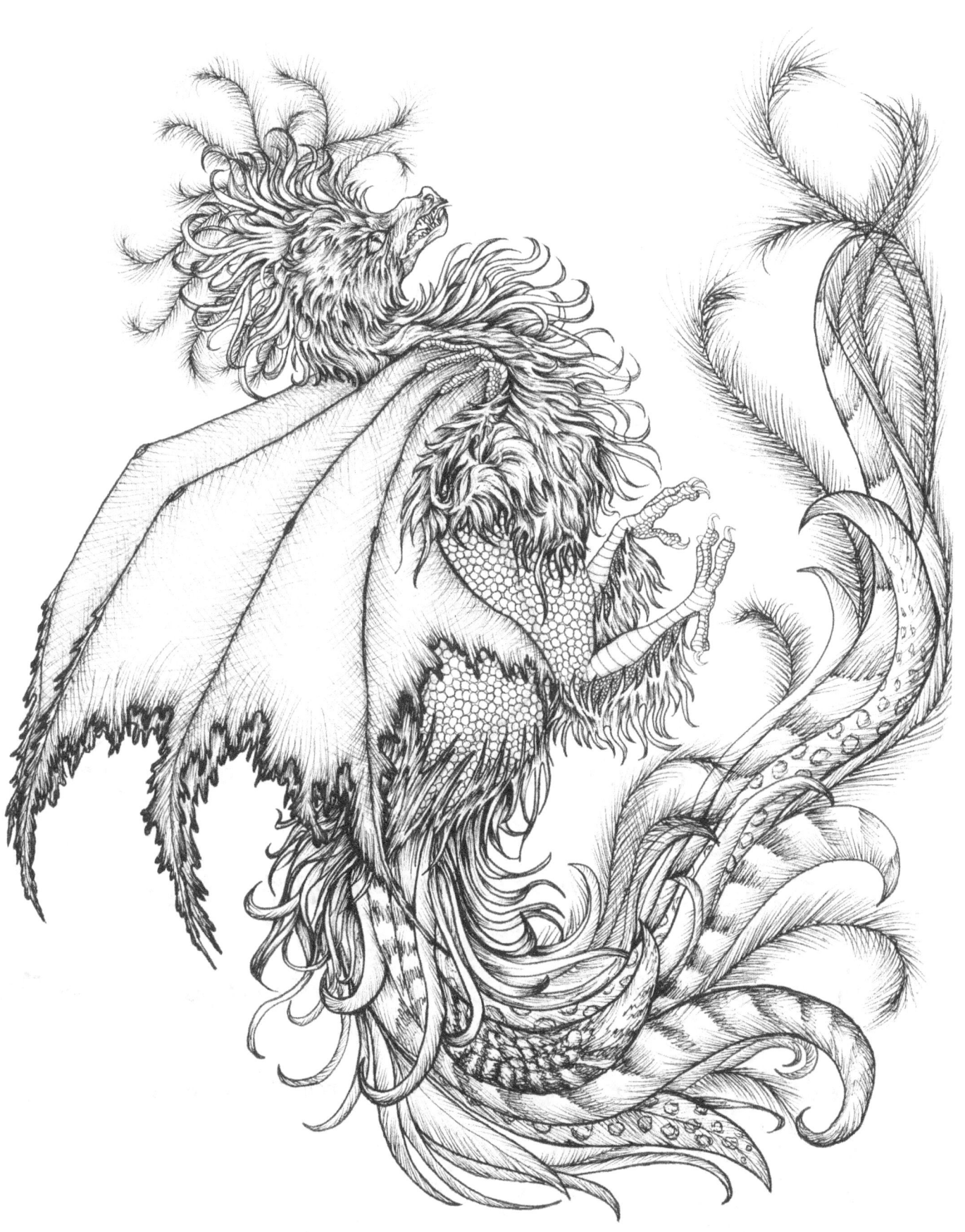

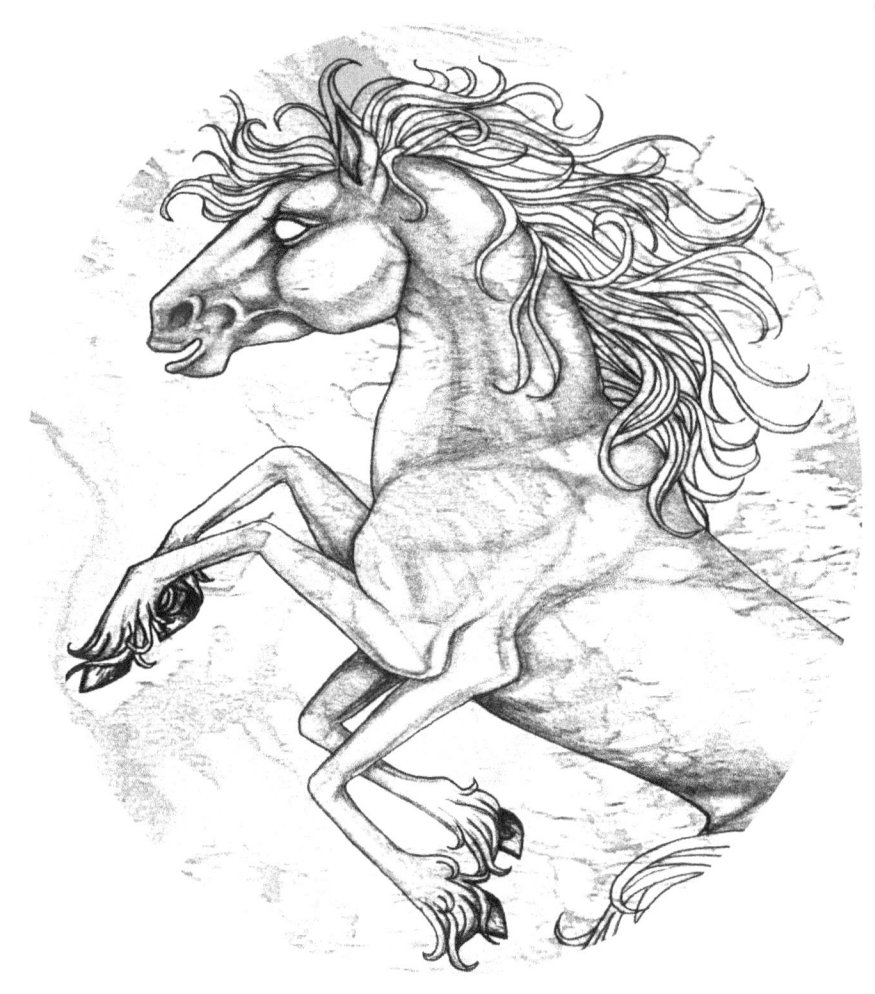

For more information on all things Keyesay please follow me at my facebook artist page:

https://www.facebook.com/keyesaysfineart

Online store: https://www.etsy.com/shop/KeyesaysVisualArt

Also all other social media sites look for "Keyesay"

www.ingramcontent.com/pod-product-compliance
Lightning Source LLC
Chambersburg PA
CBHW081415170526
45166CB00010B/3352